EARLY AMERICAN FAMILY

Meet the Allens
in Whaling Days

by John J. Loeper

BENCHMARK BOOKS

MARSHALL CAVENDISH
NEW YORK

Benchmark Books
Marshall Cavendish Corporation
99 White Plains Road
Tarrytown, New York 10591-9001

Illustrations by James Watling
Musical score and arrangement by Jerry Silverman
Map by Rodica Prato
Photo research by Matthew J. Dudley
The photographs in this book are used by permission and through the courtesy of:
The Kendall Whaling Museum, Sharon, Mass. USA: 10-11. *The Image Bank:* Steve
Dunwell, 13(left), 22, 33, 40; Michael Melford, 41, 58; Erik Leigh Simmons, 54;
Paul Loven, 61; Steve Bronstein, back cover. *Mystic Seaport Museum:* 13 (right),
19. *Peabody Essex Museum:* 18. *Old Dartmouth Historical Society-New Bedford
Whaling Museum:* 24, 26, 30, 38. *Leslie M. Newman:* 35.

Printed in Hong Kong
1   3   5   6   4   2

Library of Congress Cataloging-in-Publication Data
Loeper, John J.   Meet the Allens in whaling days/ John J. Loeper.
p.   cm. — (Early American family)
Includes bibliographical references and index.
Summary: Describes what life was like for a family on Nantucket in 1827,
including home, school, religion, and the father's expedition on a whaling ship.
ISBN 0-7614-0842-8 (lib. bdg.)
1. Nantucket (Mass.)—Biography—Juvenile literature. 2. Whaling—
Massachusetts—Nantucket—History—19th century—Juvenile literature.
3. Nantucket (Mass.)—Social life and customs—Juvenile literature.
4. Allen family—Juvenile literature. I. Title. II. Series: Loeper, John J.
Early American family.
F72.N2L64   1999   974.4'9703'0922   [B]—DC21   97-27963   CIP
AC

To the Reader

The nineteenth century was the age of sailing ships. Great wooden vessels, their sails billowing in the wind, carried people and cargo around the world. Among these ships were the whalers.

No one knows for certain how whale oil was discovered. But someone learned that the oil from whale fat could be burned as fuel. Whale oil gave a strong, clear light and was much in demand. To satisfy this demand, whales were hunted and killed.

From about 1800 to 1850, Nantucket Island became the whaling capital of the world. Every day, ships left the island in search of whales. These expeditions were long, difficult, and dangerous. Yet for hundreds of families, whaling was a way of life.

This is the story of one such family called the Allens. They lived on Nantucket. The island is a bustling community today. The Allens are long gone. Let's go back now and see how they lived during whaling days.

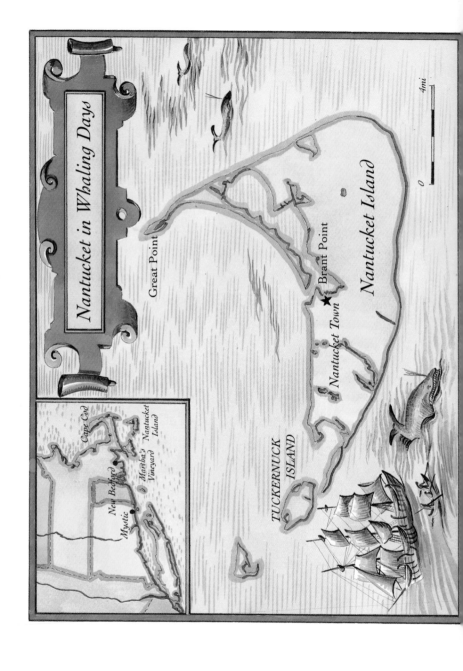

Nantucket in Whaling Days

Great Point

Brant Point

★ Nantucket Town

Nantucket Island

TUCKERNUCK
ISLAND

0   4mi

Cape Cod

New Bedford

Mystic

Martha's
Vineyard

Nantucket
Island

On a foggy September afternoon in 1827, the whaling ship *Clarkson* glided out of Nantucket harbor, leaving behind the island's mist-covered hills and rooftops. Nantucket, which lay thirty miles off the coast of Massachusetts, was often shrouded in fog. Perhaps that was why people called the island "the little gray lady of the Atlantic."

The *Clarkson* was bound for the waters of the South Pacific. The whaler would be gone for many months, perhaps as long as a year.

Standing on shore watching it leave were Hannah Allen and her two sons, Ben and Joseph. They waved, bidding farewell to the big ship. The faint figure of a man on deck waved in

On a foggy September afternoon in 1827, the whaling ship
Clarkson *glided out of Nantucket harbor.*

response. This was Joseph Allen, the captain of the *Clarkson*.

"Father will be gone again for my birthday," Ben said to his mother. Mrs. Allen took his hand and gazed at what now seemed to her a toy boat riding the slow swells of the sea.

"He can't help it, Ben," she said. "When a voyage is planned, your father must go."

"He was home for *my* birthday," boasted Joseph. "He gave me a gold coin. This will be the third year he has missed yours!"

"Don't tease your little brother," Mrs. Allen scolded. "Now, it's time for us to go home. I want both of you to finish your lessons before supper."

The three walked back into town over streets paved with cobblestones. Nantucket Town nestled on a low hill near the harbor. Gray shingled houses lined the narrow, winding streets. Here and there, the Allens passed the handsome new houses of ship owners and merchants. In the distance they heard the cries of sea gulls as they swooped low over the water, looking for fish.

Nantucket is a small island, only three miles

wide and fifteen miles long. Before whaling days, the islanders mostly farmed and raised sheep. The first settlers came from Massachusetts. One of Captain Allen's ancestors was among them. The Allen name was well known on Nantucket. An Allen served as the coroner and deputy sheriff. Another Allen was the collector and inspector of customs. Both were distant cousins of the captain.

The story is told that some early settlers were standing on a hilltop watching the spouting of whales out at sea. "There," said one, "is the pasture where our children's grandchildren will farm." This prediction came to pass. By 1800, whaling was Nantucket's main occupation.

At first, whaling was done offshore. But as the whales grew scarce, hunters had to go farther afield. Before too long they were sailing to faraway places. In 1821, Captain Allen took the *Maro* all the way to Japan, and his was the first whaling vessel to reach Honolulu.

Whaling ships, compared to merchant vessels, were rather small. They were stout but had a grace and beauty all their own. Unlike

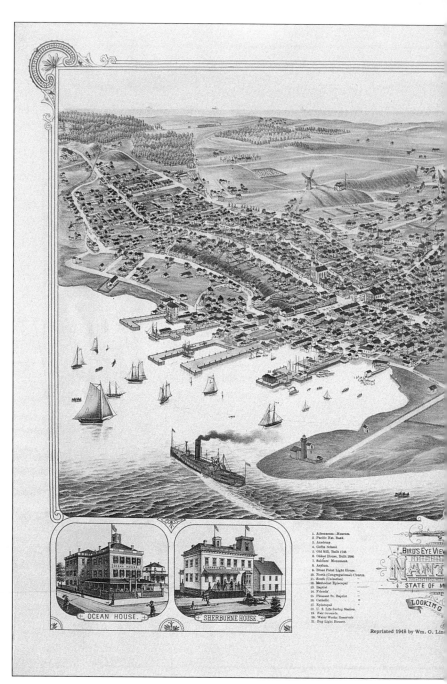

1. Athenæum—Museum.
2. Pacific Nat. Bank.
3. Academy.
4. Coffin School.
5. Old Mill, Built 1746.
6. Oldest House, Built 1686.
7. Soldiers' Monument.
8. Asylum.
9. Brant Point Light House.
10. North (Congregational) Church.
11. South (Unitarian) "
12. Methodist Episcopal "
13. Baptist "
14. Friends' "
15. Pleasant St. Baptist "
16. Catholic "
17. Episcopal "
18. U. S. Life Saving Station.
19. Fair Grounds.
20. Water Works Reservoir.
21. Bug Light Houses.

OCEAN HOUSE.

SHERBURNE HOUSE.

BIRD'S EYE VIEW
NANT
STATE OF M
LOOKING

Reprinted 1948 by Wm. O. Lin

Nantucket Town nestled on a low hill near the harbor.

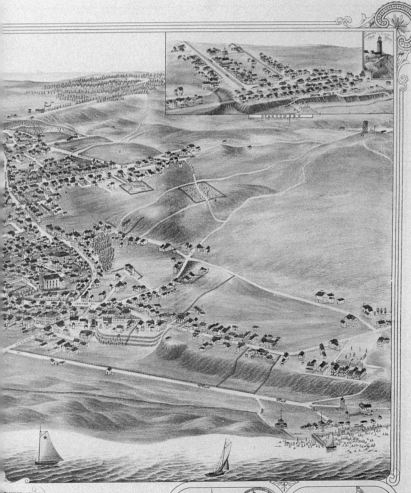

THE TOWN OF
NANTUCKET
MASSACHUSETTS.

FROM THE SOUTHWEST

, Lincoln Lane, Hingham, Mass.

SPRINGFIELD HOUSE.

OCEAN VIEW HOUSE,
SCONSET BEACH.

merchant ships, whalers had to keep their forward deck clear so that space could be given to the business of cutting and rendering, or melting down, whale fat. The galley, living quarters, and wheel clustered at the rear of the ship. Officers and crews of larger ships often referred to whalers with contempt as "butcher shops."

Whaling was a business rich in profits. Besides oil, these huge animals provided meat and whalebone. From the bones came buttons, handles, umbrella frames, knitting needles, corset stays, and dozens of other household items. The oil, made by melting whale fat, or blubber, was used for lighting. The whale oil lamp had replaced the candle. It gave a much brighter light. Nantucket whale oil lit the homes and streets of New York, London, Paris, and Rome. The island supplied the world with over a half million barrels of oil each year.

The people of Nantucket grew wealthy building whaling ships, hunting whales, and selling whale products. The owner of a ship hired a captain and crew for each expedition. Everyone, from captain to cabin boy, received

From the bones came buttons, handles, umbrella frames . . . and dozens of other household items.

The whale oil lamp had replaced the candle.

a share of the bounty. A "greasy" voyage, rich in whale oil, brought a huge sum of money. After the owner's, the captain's share was the largest. It might amount to several thousand dollars, an enormous amount in those days. This could buy a large house and bring a comfortable way of life.

The Allen family lived in a three-story white house in Nantucket Town. Its windows were framed by dark green shutters, and a porch ran along the front. Inside, a wide staircase divided the rooms, and on the roof was a railed platform called a widow's walk. Widow's walks gave access to the chimney. They also offered lookouts for sea widows—wives whose husbands had gone to sea. Women could stand on these walkways and scan the horizon for a returning ship.

The Allen home and other houses on Nantucket were filled with souvenirs of faraway places. Sitting rooms might be decorated with fierce-looking masks from Tasmania, colorful porcelain bowls from China, silk scarves from Japan, and coral shells from Tahiti. There were exotic pets too. Chattering monkeys and proud peacocks lived in backyards. Green and blue parrots squawked at visitors from perches in entrance halls, and brightly colored birds fluttered in cages.

"How long will father be gone this time?" Ben asked his mother as she tucked the boys in bed on the night of Captain Allen's departure.

"I don't know, Ben. It depends on the hunt. If they catch whales early on, he will be home within a few months. If not, the voyage will take longer."

"He may be gone for years and years," Joseph added, as he climbed into his bed on the other side of the room he shared with his brother.

Tears welled up in Ben's eyes.

"I told you not to tease your brother, Joseph!" said Mrs. Allen sternly. "Your father will not be away for years and years. With luck the *Clarkson* will return by early summer."

"Can we say a prayer for father?" Ben asked his mother.

"If you would like," she answered. She bowed

The Allens lived in a three-story white house in Nantucket Town.

her head and prayed, "Lord, guard the captain's life and see him through the perils of this journey. Give him, through your bounty, a plentiful harvest of whales and bring him home safely."

"Amen!" the boys intoned together.

While Captain Allen was away, his wife took charge of his affairs. She paid the bills and made all decisions. She also used the time to go "off island." Steamships made regular runs between Nantucket and the mainland. Mrs. Allen and the two boys took the side-wheeler *Telegraph* to

Mrs. Allen and the two boys took the side-wheeler Telegraph *to the mainland and stayed with their cousins in Boston.*

Each day began with a hearty breakfast.

the mainland and stayed with their cousins in Boston. Ben and Joseph always looked forward to seeing their relatives and taking in the sights and sounds of the big city.

On the island, the family routine continued as usual. Each day began with a hearty breakfast, often a bowl of hot cereal followed by bread and eggs. The shops on the island were packed with goods. Ships came daily from the mainland carrying fresh meats and dairy products, and seafood was plentiful. Local farmers grew fruits and vegetables, which were canned and stored for use during the winter.

The main meal of the day was served at noon, followed by a light supper at five o'clock. Mrs. Allen liked to cook and was famous for her snickerdoodles. This is the recipe she used:

Snickerdoodles

2 cups sugar
1 cup softened butter
2 eggs
¼ cup milk
1 teaspoon vanilla

3½ cups flour
½ teaspoon baking soda
½ teaspoon cream of tartar
½ teaspoon salt
1 cup chopped walnuts

Cream sugar and butter in a bowl. Add eggs. Beat well. Blend in milk and vanilla.

Mix together flour, baking soda, cream of tartar, and salt. Stir this into the creamed mixture. Blend in chopped walnuts.

Form dough into small balls. Place balls on greased cookie sheet. Flatten balls with sugared bottom of a tumbler. Bake at 375 degrees for ten to twelve minutes.

"Would you like snickerdoodles or a cake for your birthday?" Mrs. Allen asked Ben one morning at breakfast.

"Snickerdoodles!" Ben answered.

"Then that's what you shall have," Mrs. Allen replied with a smile.

"Did father leave me a present?" Ben asked.

Mrs. Allen looked at her eight-year-old son. "No, Ben, he did not. I'm sorry."

"But he promised me something special! Are you sure he didn't leave anything for me?" Ben insisted.

"I'm sure, Ben," his mother said.

"Don't worry," Joseph piped up. "I'll buy you a present with my gold coin. Would you like a toy ship?"

"No, I wouldn't," Ben sulked.

"You want to be a sailor someday, don't you?" Joseph asked. Ben nodded.

"Then you can start by learning how to sail a toy ship."

"I think that's a splendid idea," Mrs. Allen added. "And I will give you a sailor suit!"

Ben's face finally broke into a smile.

On Nantucket every boy wanted to be a sailor, and every girl wanted to marry one. Some Nantucket girls vowed never to marry a man

"Would you like a toy ship?" Joseph asked Ben.

who had not been to sea.

"When I get my sailor suit, may I wear it to school?" Ben asked.

"I suppose you want to impress Ruth Webb," Joseph teased. "She will want to sit next to you in class."

"If Mr. Freeman does not object," his mother interrupted.

Ruth Webb was the same age as Ben and lived on the next street. Her father owned the whaler *Messenger*.

"When she sees you in your sailor suit she will want you to captain the *Messenger*," Joseph continued to tease.

"I hope both of you boys end up as ship's captains," Mrs. Allen said. "But it takes more than a sailor suit to captain a ship! First, please Mr. Freeman and finish school. There will be plenty of time later to think about girls and ships!"

Mr. Freeman was known as the terror of the Quaker school and as the king of his classroom. The two Allen boys attended the Quaker school, since the Allen family belonged to the Society of Friends, as the Quakers were also known.

During the early years of the nineteenth century the island had many schools. There was the Fragment school for the poor, so named because fragments of cloth were donated to make clothing for the children. There were Cent schools. A few cents was the cost of tuition for the not-so-rich. There was a dancing school, a singing school, a writing school, a business school, and a "Negro" school. (Black children were not allowed to go to school with white children.) The Quaker school was considered the best.

The Society of Friends practiced a simple form of worship. They believed in praying without a minister. A Quaker meeting began in silence. When members were moved to speak, they did so. Anyone, the Quakers taught, could be inspired to preach and pray.

The two Allen boys attended the Quaker school.

In the nineteenth century more than half the people on Nantucket Island were Quakers. They dressed plainly in sober grays and browns. The women wore long skirts, shawls, and big bonnets. The men wore plain suits and broad-brimmed hats. Children dressed like their parents and were supposed to behave like them too. Quakers did not show strong emotion in public and frowned on frivolous behavior.

On Sunday, which the Quakers called First Day, children sat quietly through the long meeting. At the First Day meeting following the *Clarkson*'s departure, an elderly man offered a prayer for the men at sea. There were few men in the congregation. Most men and older boys were away at sea. "Let us pray," he said, "for gentle winds and a good harvest of whales."

Mrs. Allen and the boys lowered their heads along with the others. They all knew the dangers facing the absent men. Some might not return.

Whaling was not for the weak or timid. When the cry went out, "Whale ho! Thar she blows!"

The women wore long skirts, shawls, and big bonnets.

The men wore plain suits and broad-brimmed hats.

Children dressed like their parents and were supposed to behave like them too.

the sailors rushed to lower the smaller whale boats from the ship, clambered in, and took off after the whale.

When a boat neared the whale, the harpooner hurled a barbed, iron spear into the whale's side. The harpoon, which was attached to a long rope, was not meant to kill the whale but to fasten it to the boat. The harpooned whale took off at great speed in pain and fright. The boat was dragged along in what was called a "Nantucket sleigh ride."

The wounded whale rolled and tumbled in the water. It lashed out in rage. Often it leaped open-jawed into the air. Its huge tail slapped the whaling boats with the force of a tidal wave. Boats were known to capsize, and men were tossed into the sea. With luck, the whale soon tired, and the men finished it off with an eight-foot spear.

The carcass was towed back to the ship, where the blubber (the layer of fat beneath the skin) was removed and rendered in big vats. The stench from the boiling blubber was terrible. A whaling captain's wife described the

When a boat neared the whale, the harpooner hurled a barbed,
iron spear into the whale's side.

The stench from the boiling blubber was terrible.

process in a journal she kept during the voyage:

> *The carcass of the dead animal fills the deck. The men boil out the blubber in big pots. When it cools, they get into the pots and squish the blubber with their feet. They are often up to their knees in oil.*

The whale was not the only casualty. The people of Nantucket shared many frightening stories, such as that of the *Essex.* One day, without warning, a large whale swam toward the ship. It struck the vessel with such force that the men on board were knocked down. The ship trembled and came to a stop. The whale dived under the ship and struck again. The *Essex* was badly damaged, and the captain ordered his men to abandon ship.

From the whale boats they watched the ship roll over on its side. The damage done, the whale took off into the high seas. It had been a successful voyage, and hundreds of barrels of whale oil were on board. The barrels broke open, and the oil spread over the water. Miles and miles from land, the men stayed afloat with few supplies for many months. Only three survived. They were rescued by a passing whale ship, the *Dauphin* of Nantucket.

The fate of the *Essex* caused many a Nantuck-eter to shiver in fear at the awesome strength of the whale. They remembered the *Ann Alexander* of New Bedford, rammed in mid-ocean by a sperm whale. Another whaler, the *Lydia*, had returned with her flag at half-mast. Her captain, Silas Swain, had fallen overboard and was carried underwater by a struggling whale.

Despite the danger, boys longed to go to sea. Nantucket children often sat on the docks listening to the sailors sing as they hoisted a sail or pulled in an anchor. Here is one of the sea chanteys they might have heard:

Nantucket children often sat on the docks listening to the sailors sing as they hoisted a sail or pulled in an anchor.

Greenland Fisheries

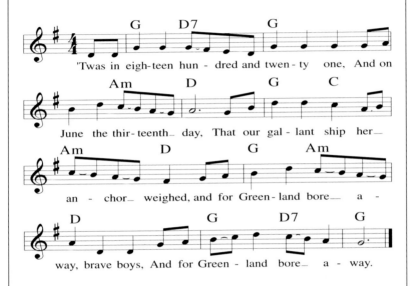

'Twas in eigh-teen hun - dred and twen - ty one, And on
June the thir - teenth_ day, That our gal - lant ship her_
an - chor_ weighed, and for Green - land bore_ a -
way, brave boys, And for Green - land bore_ a - way.

The lookout in the crosstrees stood,
With a spyglass in his hand.
"There's a whale, there's a whale, there's a whalefish," he cried,
"And she blows at every span, brave boys,
And she blows at every span."

Now the boats were launched and the men aboard,
And the whale was in full view.
Resolved was each seaman bold
To steer where the whalefish blew, brave boys,
To steer where the whalefish blew.

We struck that whale and the line paid out,
But she gave a flourish with her tail.
The boat capsized and four men were drowned,
And we never caught that whale, brave boys,
And we never caught that whale.

"To lose the whale," our captain said,
"It grieves my heart full sore.
But oh, to lose four gallant men,
It grieves me ten times more, brave boys,
It grieves me ten times more."

Oh, Greenland is a dreadful place,
A land that's never green.
Where there's ice and snow and the whalefishes blow,
And the daylight's seldom seen, brave boys,
And the daylight's seldom seen.

Ben and Joseph longed for the day when they could set sail. The sea was in their blood. Not only were the Allens seafaring men, but their mother's brothers were sailors too. They would start as cabin boys, cleaning quarters and polishing boots. Then they would become seamen, and after that, perhaps a captain!

"I am thinking to ask Mr. Starbuck to take me on as a cabin boy," Joseph confided in Ben as they lay in their beds early one morning. "After all, I will soon be twelve years old." Mr. Starbuck owned their father's ship and was very wealthy. He had built three identical brick houses for each of his sons. Islanders called the houses "the three brothers."

"I want to be a sailor, too!" Ben cried. "I'll be nine on my birthday."

"You're too little to be a sailor," Joseph said. Then he began to recite: "An old sailor man and Pinch Me went off to sea in a boat. The old sailor man jumped overboard. Who was left afloat?"

"Pinch Me!" shouted Ben. And Joseph hopped out of bed and pinched him.

"Boys!" their mother called. "Please get

Mr. Starbuck had built three identical brick houses for each of his sons.

dressed and come down here right away." They grabbed their clothes, threw on their shirts and trousers, and raced to the stairs.

"I have a letter from your father," she told them. "Mrs. Ellis, whose husband commands the *Washington*, brought it to me. He just returned from a voyage. Your father met up with him in Honolulu and gave him this letter for us."

Mrs. Allen broke the seal and unfolded her husband's letter. She began to read:

Dear Family,

We encountered a fierce storm at the tip of South America but rounded the Horn without any loss of life. We took eight whales off the coast of Chile and have over eight hundred barrels of oil stored in the hold. Another five or six hundred barrels will make this voyage eminently successful.

Yesterday I had to take off a man's leg. A barrel fell on it and crushed it beyond repair. I dislike this part of my duties.

I miss you all and long to see you. We hope to return home by August. I will miss Ben's birthday again but will make up for my neglect. I have a special surprise for him.

With love,
Your Father

Ben's face glowed with happiness. "What do you suppose the surprise is?" he asked his mother.

"We will have to wait and see," she replied.

Mrs. Allen worried about her husband. She knew the months of command weighed heavily on him. The captain of the ship was responsible for the safekeeping of all his men. This meant, she knew, serving as the ship's doctor as well as its captain. And illness and accidents were commonplace. Sailors suffered from fevers and chills. Every captain carried a medicine chest filled with remedies and instruments. Occasionally he had to pull a tooth or set a broken bone. There were times when a captain had to perform crude operations, as Captain Allen had in removing a sailor's leg. And there were deaths on board. Then the captain became a minister. He conducted a service, and the dead body was lowered into the sea.

A sailor's life was, to many minds, rather grim. The men lived mostly on hardtack (dried bread) and dried fish. The ship carried a supply of rice, flour, potatoes, and dried beans, but the

A sailor's life was, to many minds, rather grim.

daily diet was dull and changed little for
weeks on end. Occasionally a few chickens
were brought on board, but the hens' eggs were
reserved for the captain.

Diary entries made by Laura Jernegan, who
accompanied her father on a whaling expedition, give an idea of the monotony of the daily
fare:

> *"We had baked potatoes and biscuits for supper."*
> *"Today's dinner was potatoes and beans."*
> *"For supper we had boiled potatoes and rice."*

Someone once wrote that a newspaper advertisement for help on a whaling expedition should read like this:

MEN WANTED FOR HAZARDOUS JOURNEY

Uncertain wages, poor food, hard work,
uncomfortable quarters, constant danger,
safe return not guaranteed.

Family life had its daily routines, and so the months slipped quietly by. Joseph and Ben kept up with their lessons. They studied reading, writing, arithmetic, and Bible history. School was held at the Quaker meetinghouse for a few hours each day except Sunday. When not in school, the boys sailed their kites, picked wild berries, climbed sand dunes, or watched the big sailing ships come and go in the harbor. Nantucket was home port to more than one hundred and twenty-five sailing ships. Workers hurried to the docks each morning to service the ships, and warehouses stored with supplies lined the wharves. There was always something

Joseph and Ben studied reading, writing, arithmetic, and Bible history.

going on, always something to watch.

Ben celebrated his birthday on April 12. All day long the delicious aromas of special foods filled the house. That afternoon a birthday supper was served in the Allen dining room. A bouquet of early daffodils from the back garden

When not in school, the boys sailed their kites, picked wild berries, climbed sand dunes, or watched the big sailing ships come and go in the harbor.

sat on the sideboard, and on the table were platters of cold meats, puddings, pies, tarts, and, of course, snickerdoodles. A polished silver pot held hot chocolate.

Mrs. Allen invited several of the boys' friends as well as Ruth Webb and her mother.

"Perhaps you should show Ruth your birthday present," Mrs. Allen told Ben with a mischievous smile. Ben took his sailor suit from its box and held it up for all to admire. It was white with blue and gold piping. Its brass buttons had tiny anchors stamped on them.

"I shall call you Admiral Allen," Ruth exclaimed when she saw it. Ben blushed with embarrassment and pleasure.

"And here is the boat I gave Ben!" Joseph called out. He held up a toy boat with tiny white sails.

"How long has your husband been gone?" Mrs. Webb asked her hostess.

"Eight months," Mrs. Allen answered. "I pray that he's safe."

"Mr. Webb told me that the *Clarkson* and the

Messenger had a gamming a while back and that all is well."

When two ships met at sea they came close together. The crews visited back and forth in their whaling boats. They ate a meal together, exchanged news, and told stories. This time of camaraderie was known as a gamming.

"What good news you bring me," Mrs. Allen replied. "But the best news will be word that the *Clarkson* has returned!"

On August 25, 1828, word *did* arrive at the Allen home. The *Clarkson* had been sighted by another ship about one day's journey from Nantucket. On hearing the news, the boys and their mother hurried up to the widow's walk and scanned the horizon.

"I can't sight it," Mrs. Allen announced, holding a brass spyglass to her eye. "The ship is too far out. But the captain should be home tomorrow!"

That night, Ben and Joseph lay awake in their beds. There was so much to think about. Their

"And here is the boat I gave Ben!" Joseph called out.

father would be back with them tomorrow. Had he changed? Joseph wondered. Perhaps he had grown a beard. And Ben could think of nothing but his promised surprise. They listened to the sounds entering the open bedroom window: the creaking of wooden masts coming from the waterfront, footsteps on the street below, the distant call of one sailor to another, the chirping of crickets. A salt breeze scented with bayberry blew into the room and finally lulled them to sleep.

The next morning the town crier called out the news.

"A ship is coming!" he cried. "The *Clarkson*! A ship is coming!"

The news spread from house to house. The islanders eagerly searched the horizon from their widow's walks to catch a glimpse of the distant vessel. Others hastened to the wharf to witness her approach. Among them were Mrs. Allen and the boys. They watched the ship coming closer. She was riding low in the water. That meant that her hold was filled with casks of whale oil.

"They have had greasy luck!" the old whaling men said.

Arms reached from the jostling crowd to catch the lines tossed by scruffy, suntanned whalers. Captain Allen was the first to disembark. He had grown a beard and lost some weight. Mrs. Allen looked at him with admiration. He was still the handsome sailor she had married. She thought of the old cliché: absence makes the heart grow fonder. It was true; she had missed her husband terribly. Even now at the moment of his return, she dreaded the day he would set out on another voyage. He ran to embrace her. Then he put his arms around the two boys and pulled them close. He smelled of whale oil and the sea. He looked at his family and smiled. They were together again.

That night the boys listened to their father's tales of the journey. They drank lemonade and ate cookies. Mrs. Allen had made a batch of snickerdoodles. Before going to bed, Ben brought up the matter of his surprise.

"Tomorrow, son," the captain promised. "You'll see it tomorrow!"

Captain Allen was the first to disembark.

The next day, at his father's insistence, Ben dressed in his sailor suit. Then the entire family set off.

"Where are we going, father?" Ben asked.

"To Brant Point. I have something to show you."

"Is it my present?" Ben asked.

"Could be," his father replied with a smile. "Could be!"

Reaching Brant Point, they walked out onto a short wooden dock. In the water was a newly built skiff. The long narrow boat was painted bright blue and had a small red sail. The *Clarkson*'s carpenter had built it for the captain while at sea.

"What do you think of it, Joseph?" the captain asked.

"It's a beauty!" Joseph exclaimed as he jumped on board.

"Ben, I want you to look at the prow very carefully," the captain ordered.

Ben scampered ahead to examine the front of the boat. There in gleaming gold letters was the boat's name: *Benjamin Allen.*

Ben beamed. "Is it mine, father?" he asked.

"Of course," he answered. "It has your name on it!"

"You may be the captain of my ship," Ben said to his brother, who was still on board. "But remember that I am the owner and I'm in charge!"

Two men who were walking by stopped to admire the boat.

"A seaworthy vessel if I ever saw one!" one of the men remarked.

"Are you planning to hunt whales with her?" the other asked Ben.

"I might," Ben replied. "If so, would you like to sign on as crew members?"

Everyone laughed.

"Thank you, father," Ben said. "This is the best birthday present ever!"

"Now for another surprise," Captain Allen announced. "Your mother has made ice cream, and we are all going home to celebrate your new boat."

"Hooray for the *Benjamin Allen!*" the boys shouted together.

"Thank you, father," Ben said. "This is the best birthday present ever!"

Ben and Joseph both became sailors. Joseph left home the following year, when he turned thirteen. Ben, too, went to sea at thirteen years old. He chased his first whale before he turned sixteen, and Joseph went on to become a captain like his father.

As the years went by, the world changed. Kerosene, refined from petroleum, replaced whale oil in lamps throughout the world. It was less expensive and easier to produce. Steamships took the place of sailing vessels, and

The old houses still loom over Nantucket's misty streets.

Nantucket soon lost its position as a commercial port. The age of whaling was over.

The old houses still loom over Nantucket's misty streets, now filled with tourists. The warehouses along the docks have been turned into art galleries, museums, and gift shops. Times have changed. Yet the "little gray lady of the Atlantic" holds many reminders of days gone by.

Allen Family Tree

The Allen name is so ancient that its origin is lost in the mists of unrecorded history. The name has a Saxon root meaning, "loved by all."

Allen is a common English name much like Smith or Jones. Because it is so common and there were and are so many people by the name, it is difficult to trace an ancestry.

The first Allen in the New World was John Allen, an English Puritan. He fled from his home in 1596 and settled in Massachusetts around 1639. Most of the American Allens are his descendants.

Captain Joseph Allen of Nantucket was most likely descended from the Allens of Harwich, Massachusetts.

About 1729, William and Suzanna Allen of Harwich had a son named John. As an adult, John married Hannah Paine and moved to Nantucket in 1760. They had eleven children. One of the eleven, John, was the father of Joseph Allen.

Captain Allen married Hannah Baldwin in June 1814. They had two sons: Joseph, born in 1816, and Benjamin, born in 1819.

In the 1790 United States census, there were hundreds of Allens listed. Today, there are over five hundred thousand Allens living in the United States. The Allen family is woven into the fabric of American history.

The Allens of Nantucket

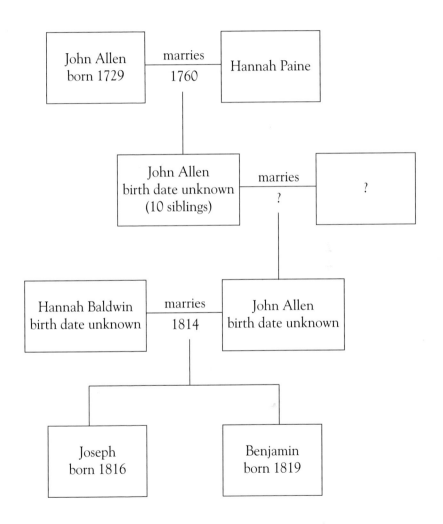

John Allen
born 1729

marries
1760

Hannah Paine

John Allen
birth date unknown
(10 siblings)

marries
?

?

Hannah Baldwin
birth date unknown

marries
1814

John Allen
birth date unknown

Joseph
born 1816

Benjamin
born 1819

Places to Visit

To learn more about seafaring and whaling ships, here
are some places to visit.

Mystic Seaport, Mystic, Connecticut
A re-creation of a New England seafaring village
with nearly sixty museum buildings and ships.
There are shops and craft demonstrations.

Nantucket Historic District, Nantucket, Massachusetts
Numerous fine houses are to be found on Main
Street, between Centre Street and Monument
Square. The Nantucket Historical Association has

a whaling museum housed in a former factory near the wharf.

New Bedford Historic District, New Bedford, Mass. New Bedford was also a major whaling port. There are many old houses and buildings still standing. A Whaling Museum on Johnny Cake Hill contains the world's largest model whaling ship, along with paintings of whale hunts and whaling tools.

Books to Read

Here are some titles you might enjoy, which bring whales and the exciting days of the great whalers alive.

Fiction

Adams, Pam. *Wally Whale & Friends.* Auburn, ME: Childs Play, 1981.

Carrick, Carol. *Whaling Days.* New York: Houghton Mifflin, 1996.

Crofford, Emily. *Born in the Year of Courage.* Minneapolis: Lerner Group, 1991.

Melville, Herman. *Moby Dick.* Ashland, OH: Landoll, 1995.

Tokuda, Wendy and Hall, Richard. *Humphrey the Lost Whale.* Torrance, CA: Heian International, 1986.

Nonfiction

Kalman, Bobbie. *Arctic Whales & Whaling.* New York: Crabtree Publishing, 1988.

Meadowcroft, Enid. *When Nantucketmen Went Whaling.* Champaign, IL: Garrard, 1966.

Stanley, Diane. *The True Adventures of Daniel Hall.* New York: Dial, 1995.

Stein, Conrad. *The Story of New England Whalers.* Chicago: Children's Press, 1982.

Zonderman, Jon. *A Whaling Captain.* Vero Beach, FL: Rourke, 1994.

Index

Page numbers for illustrations are in boldface.

About the Author

J. Loeper was born in Ashland, Pennsylvania. He has been a teacher, counselor, and school administrator. He has both taught and studied in Europe.

Mr. Loeper has contributed articles and poems to newspapers, journals, and national magazines. He is the author of more than a dozen books for young readers, all dealing with American history, and an active member of several historical societies. The *Chicago Sun* called him the "young reader's expert on Americana."

Mr. Loeper is also an exhibiting artist and has illustrated one of the books he authored. He and his wife divide their time between Connecticut and Florida.